EXPANDED EDITION
Grade 2

T0193005

The *Wind and Water* lesson is part of the
Picture-Perfect STEM program K–2 written by the
program authors and includes lessons from their
award-winning series.

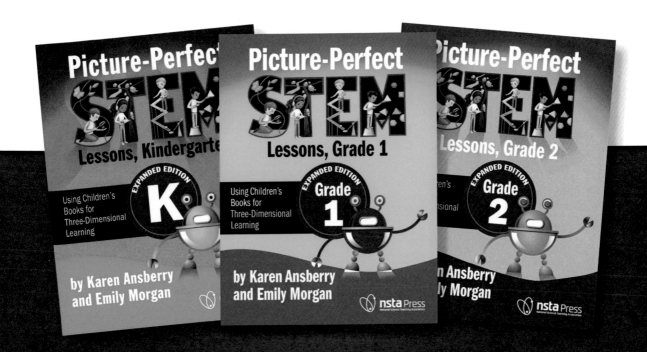

Wind and Water

Description

Students explore the phenomenon that wind and water can change the shape of the land and remove soil. They explore natural solutions that can help control erosion, such as planting trees and grass, as well as technologies, such as building levees and installing erosion control fabric. Finally, they compare multiple solutions to an erosion problem and describe one that they think will be the best.

Alignment with the *Next Generation Science Standards*

Performance Expectations

2-ESS1-1: Use information from several sources to provide evidence that Earth events can occur quickly or slowly.

2-ESS2-1: Compare multiple solutions designed to slow or prevent wind or water from changing the shape of the land.

K-2-ETS1-3: Analyze data from tests of two objects designed to solve the same problem to compare the strengths and weaknesses of how each performs.

Science and Engineering Practices	Disciplinary Core Ideas	Crosscutting Concept
Analyzing and Interpreting Data Use observations (firsthand or from media) to describe patterns and/or relationships in the natural and designed world in order to answer scientific questions and solve problems. **Constructing Explanations and Designing Solutions** Compare multiple solutions to a problem.	**ESS1.C: The History of Planet Earth** Some events happen very quickly; others occur very slowly over a time period much longer than one can observe. **ESS2.A: Earth Materials and Systems** Wind and water can change the shape of the land. **ETS1.C: Optimizing the Design Solution** Because there is always more than one possible solution to a problem, it is useful to compare and test designs.	**Stability and Change** Things may change slowly or rapidly.

Note: The activities in this lesson will help students move toward the performance expectations listed, which is the goal after multiple activities. However, the activities will not by themselves be sufficient to reach the performance expectations.

Featured Picture Books

TITLE: ***Kate, Who Tamed the Wind***
AUTHOR: **Liz Garton Scanlon**
ILLUSTRATOR: **Lee White**
PUBLISHER: **Schwartz and Wade Books**
YEAR: **2018**
GENRE: **Story**
SUMMARY: *A resourceful girl named Kate has a neighbor who lives at the top of a very steep hill. The wind is blowing everything away, including the clothes on his clothesline, the shutters on his house, and even his words. Kate solves the man's problem with the wind by designing an environmentally sound solution: planting trees.*

TITLE: ***How Do Wind and Water Change Earth?***
AUTHOR: **Natalie Hyde**
PUBLISHER: **Crabtree Publishing**
YEAR: **2015**
GENRE: **Non-Narrative Information**
SUMMARY: *This nonfiction book defines weathering and erosion, describes fast and slow changes that build up and wear down landforms, and identifies ways that water changes Earth through rivers, tides, landslides, freeze/thaw cycles, and glaciers.*

Time Needed

This lesson will take several class periods. Suggested scheduling is as follows:

Session 1: **Engage** with *Kate, Who Tamed the Wind* Read-Aloud and **Explore** with Wind and Water Change Earth's Surface Media Gallery

Session 2: **Explore** with Wind and Water Model

Session 3: **Explain** with *How Do Wind and Water Change Earth?* Cloze and Read-Aloud and Erosion Problems

Session 4: **Elaborate** with Erosion Solutions Journal and **Evaluate** with Comparing Solutions

Session 5 and beyond: **Evaluate** with A Local Erosion Problem

Materials

Note: Throughout the lesson, a computer and a whiteboard or projector will be needed to display images.

For Wind and Water Model (per class)

- Large, shallow, clear plastic tub or container, approx. 40 qt. capacity
- Approx. 10 lbs. of clean, damp play sand
- Small toy house or upside-down plastic cup

- 6 plastic hand pumps
- 6 plastic squeeze bottles (12–16 oz.)
- 24 miniature plastic trees (the kind used for cupcake décor or crafts)
- 6 safety goggles
- Water supply
- (Optional) Stopwatch or cell phone timer

For How Do Wind and Water Change Earth? *Cloze and Read-Aloud*

- Scissors
- Tape or glue

Student Pages

- Wind and Water Cloze
- Erosion Solutions Journal (stapled)
- STEM Everywhere

Background for Teachers

Scientists have evidence that Earth is at least 4.5 billion years old. During this long span of time, Earth's surface has been in a state of constant change. Both constructive and destructive forces of nature have changed Earth's surface throughout its history. *Constructive forces,* such as volcanic eruptions, crustal deformation, and deposition, build up mountains and landmasses. *Destructive forces,* such as weathering and erosion, wear away Earth's surface. *Weathering* refers to the physical breakdown of rock caused by factors such as water, wind, freeze-thaw cycles, and plant roots, or chemical breakdown such as the wearing away of rock surfaces by acid rain. *Erosion* occurs when weathered rock and soil fragments are transported to another place by wind, water, or ice. *Deposition* occurs when the materials are dropped in another place.

Most changes to Earth's surface caused by weathering and erosion happen very slowly over many years. For example, slow-moving glaciers can take hundreds or thousands of years to create valleys and other landforms through erosion. Geologists estimate it took the Colorado River 5–6 million years to carve out the Grand Canyon. However, some changes can occur in a matter of minutes, hours, or days. Riverbank erosion can happen quickly during a flood or storm surge. A rapidly moving landslide or mudslide, triggered by heavy rain, wind, or earthquakes, can change the surface of Earth in minutes. The powerful waves, wind, and heavy rainfall caused by a strong hurricane can move massive amounts of sand away from beaches, reshaping the coastal landscape quickly. Sandstorms and dust storms can lift large amounts of sand and dust from bare, dry soils and deposit them miles away in a matter of hours.

Wind affects landscapes through a process called *wind erosion*, in which wind breaks up land and carries soil, sand, and bits of rock to other places. Wind erosion can have a devastating effect on farmland by removing fertile topsoil. Eroded soil can be deposited in waterways where it affects water quality. It can also be emitted into the air where it affects air quality.

There are a variety of methods that can control both wind and water erosion, with many more being developed. Erosion control methods protect farmland and residential landscapes from soil loss, prevent

water pollution caused by stormwater runoff, reduce habitat loss, and diminish human property damage. A natural way to prevent erosion is by planting vegetation. Plant roots hold the soil together and prevent excess movement. Tree trunks, leaves, and branches protect soil from wind. Examples include planting dune grass to protect sand dunes, planting trees in strategic places to act as windbreaks, planting cover crops, and inserting live willow stakes into the ground to hold soil in place along streambanks. Mulching with plant materials is another natural but short-term erosion control method.

Other erosion control methods include structural solutions such as earthen or concrete levees, floodwalls, retaining walls, terraces, fences, gravel, and riprap (large rocks installed in mesh where a structure or shoreline is exposed to rushing water). There are also many technologies that have been developed to control erosion, such as *erosion control fabrics* made of materials like coconut fiber, straw, or geotextiles. These fabrics protect loose soil from short-term erosion while promoting germination and plant growth for long-term erosion control. Ideally, native plants should be used in combination with erosion control fabric.

The advantages and disadvantages of any solution must be considered when planning erosion control. For example, many plastics used in erosion control are not biodegradable. Wildlife can get entangled in plastic netting, which is especially deadly to snakes. The application of larger-sized riprap makes it difficult for wildlife to move along a shoreline. Levees can fail, causing catastrophic damage. Some erosion control methods may not be aesthetically pleasing, and people often avoid adopting any solution that reduces profits, takes too long to work, or is too labor-intensive or expensive.

In this lesson, students use the science and engineering practice (SEP) of obtaining, evaluating, and communicating information as they read about the effects of wind and water erosion on soil and landforms. Then they apply the SEP of constructing explanations and designing solutions as they compare solutions to slow or prevent wind and water erosion. Students recognize the crosscutting concept (CCC) of stability and change as they learn how some changes to Earth's surface occur slowly, over many years, or rapidly, over hours or days. The idea that wind and water can change the shape of land is a foundational concept that students will build upon in later grades.

Learning Progressions

Below are the disciplinary core idea (DCI) grade band endpoints for grades K–2 and 3–5. These are provided to show how student understanding of the DCIs in this lesson will progress in future grade levels.

DCIs	Grades K–2	Grades 3–5
ESS1.C: The History of Planet Earth	• Some events happen very quickly; others occur very slowly, over a time period much longer than one can observe.	• Local, regional, and global patterns of rock formations reveal changes over time due to Earth forces such as earthquakes. The presence and location of certain fossil types indicate the order in which rock layers were formed.

Continued

DCIs	Grades K–2	Grades 3–5
ESS2.A: Earth Materials and Systems	• Wind and water can change the shape of the land..	• Rainfall helps to shape the land and affects the types of living things found in a region. Water, ice, wind, living organisms, and gravity break rocks, soils, and sediments into smaller particles and move them around.
ETS1.C: Optimizing the Design Solution	• Because there is always more than one possible solution to a problem, it is useful to compare and test designs.	• Different solutions need to be tested in order to determine which of them best solves the problem, given the criteria and the constraints.

Source: Willard, T., ed. 2015. *The NSTA quick-reference guide to the* NGSS: *Elementary school.* Arlington, VA: NSTA Press.

engage

Kate, Who Tamed the Wind Read-Aloud

Connecting to the Common Core
Reading: Literature
Key Ideas and Details: 2.1

**Inferring**

Show students the cover of *Kate, Who Tamed the Wind* and share the names of the author and illustrator. *Ask*

? What do you think the title means? (Answers will vary.)

? What does the word *tame* mean? (Answers will vary, but students may make analogies to taming an animal or use words such as *control, tone down, conquer,* etc.)

? Can you see wind? (no)

? How can you tell from the cover that it's windy there? (there are leaves in the air, the trees are bent)

**Making Connections: Text to Self**

? Have you ever lost anything to the wind? (Answers will vary.)

? Can you stop the wind from blowing? (no)

? How could you keep the wind from carrying away your things? (Answers will vary, but students may have tied things down, used rocks as paperweights, or used windbreaks such as umbrellas.)

Tell students that as you read, you would like them to listen for what the author means by "taming the wind." Read the book aloud, then *ask*

? What did the man lose to the wind? (clothes from the clothesline, shutters, boards, his hat, even his words)

? How did Kate make her plan to help the man? (She drew her ideas on the ground with chalk.)

? What was Kate's plan? (to carry trees in a wagon to the top of the hill, plant them around the man's house, and wait for them to grow)

? How did the illustrator show that much time had passed by the end of the story? (the man's beard had turned gray, Kate had grown up)

? Did Kate's plan work? How do you know? (Yes, because the neighbor's things were no longer lost to the wind.)

Synthesizing

? Now that you have heard the story, what do you think the title means? (Kate did something to "tame," or control, the wind in order to help her neighbor.)

explore

Wind and Water Change Earth's Surface Media Gallery

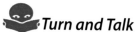
Turn and Talk

After reading, have students turn to a partner and discuss this question:

? What can wind do? (Answers may include damage homes, move or carry objects, blow down trees, and so on.)

 Then project this photo of a field in Kansas: *https://agriculture.ks.gov/images/default-source/default-album/wind-erosion.jpg?sfvrsn=f8a78ac1_0*

Ask

? What do you think is happening in the picture? (Wind is blowing away the soil from the field.)

? Why do you think that is happening? (The soil is dry, it is windy, there are no trees to block the wind, there is nothing covering the soil, there are no plants holding the soil in place, etc.)

? How do you think that affects the farmer? (The farmer's crops would not grow, or grow as well, without the topsoil.)

> **SEP: Analyzing and Interpreting Data**
> Use observations (firsthand or from media) to describe patterns and/or relationships in the natural and designed world in order to answer scientific questions and solve problems.

Tell students you are going to show some more videos and photographs of wind changing Earth's surface. Have students make observations and share them with a partner as you project the media collection called "Wind Changes Earth's Surface."

This collection features videos and photos of the following phenomena:

- Wind blowing sand on sand dunes
- Sand covering a bench
- A tornado forming
- Trees knocked down by the wind

 www.pbslearningmedia.org/resource/buac20-k2-sci-ess-windandwaterchanges/wind-and-water-change-earths-surface

Stop after sharing each example from the media collection, and *ask*

? What did you notice? (Answers will vary.)

? What do you wonder? (Answers will vary.)

? What can wind do? (move sand or soil, form a tornado, knock down trees)

? Do those things happen quickly or slowly? (Some happen quickly, some happen more slowly. Some occur in seconds, like the tornado. Others can take hours or days, like the wind blowing the sand to cover the bench. Some changes can even take many years to happen.)

Then *ask*

? What other things can change Earth's surface? (Answers will vary, but students may know about water erosion, earthquakes, volcanoes, landslides, glaciers, etc.)

Tell students that you are going to show some videos and photographs of water changing Earth's surface. Have students make observations and share them with their partner as you project the media collection called "Water Changes Earth's Surface." (Use the same web address as before, but scroll to find the "Water" gallery.)

This collection features videos and photos of the following phenomena:

- Water moving small rocks and sand along a riverbed
- A riverbank that has been worn away by water
- A mudslide caused by extreme rainfall
- Waves breaking off large pieces of land from a coastline
- Waves wearing away the underside of a coastal cliff

> **SEP: Analyzing and Interpreting Data**
> Use observations (firsthand or from media) to describe patterns and/or relationships in the natural and designed world in order to answer scientific questions and solve problems.

Stop after sharing each example from the media collection, and *ask*

? What did you notice? (Answers will vary.)

? What do you wonder? (Answers will vary.)

? What can water do? (move rocks or sand, wear away the bank of a river, cause a mudslide, break off large pieces of land from a coastline, wear away the underside of a cliff)

? Do those things happen quickly or slowly? (Some happen quickly; some happen more slowly. Some occur in seconds, like the mudslide. Others can take hours or days, like the riverbank being worn away by water. Some changes can even take many years to happen.)

Wind and Water Model

Note: This activity can be messy and is best done outside.

Pour about 10 lbs of clean, damp play sand into a long, clear plastic tub (the bigger, the better) and form it into a steep hill. Place a small toy house or an upside-down plastic cup at the peak of the hill to represent the house where Kate's neighbor lives. Press the house firmly into the sand so it doesn't move easily. Have hand pumps, squirt bottles, and a water source nearby.

Then gather students around the container, and tell them that scientists and engineers often build models to help them understand phenomena such as the effects of wind and water on Earth's surface. Have students think back to the book *Kate, Who Tamed the Wind*, and *ask*

? What does the pile of sand represent in this model? (the hill where the neighbor lived)

DEMONSTRATING THE POWER OF WIND

DEMONSTRATING THE POWER OF WATER

MODELING KATE'S SOLUTION

? What do the grains of sand represent? (soil)

? What does the model of a house represent? (the neighbor's house)

? What problem did the neighbor have? (There was too much wind.)

? How could we represent wind in our model? (Blow on the sand and the house.)

Demonstrate the power of wind by having no more than six students at a time put on safety goggles and use hand pumps to blow on the mound of sand (you may want to set a timer for 10 seconds). Make sure no one is standing "down wind." For fun, have the rest of the class make "wind sounds"!

Have the class make observations after each group of students has blown on the sand. Then *ask*

? What did you notice? (Students should notice that the "wind" blows sand away.)

? What can wind do? (blow sand/soil, carry sand/soil away, destroy landforms)

Next, demonstrate the power of water by having no more than six students at a time put on safety goggles and use squeeze bottles to squirt water on the mound of sand (you may want set a timer for 10 seconds). For fun, have the rest of the class make "rain sounds"!

Have the class make observations after each group of students has squirted water on the sand. Then *ask*

? What did you notice? (Students should notice that the water moves the sand aside to form trenches or channels and that some of the sand is carried away to the bottom of the hill by the water.)

? What can water do? (move sand/soil, carry sand/soil away, destroy landforms)

Next, ask students to think back to Kate's idea in the book *Kate, Who Tamed the Wind. Ask*

? What could we do to protect our sand hill from wearing away? (Plant something on it.)

Tell students that you can use plastic trees to represent the trees planted by Kate. (*Note*: You may need to reform the sand dune before moving forward.) Have students press the trees firmly into the sand. Then have a few more students take turns blowing air and squirting water on the sand. *Ask*

? What did you notice? (Answers will vary.)

? What was different this time? (Answers will vary.)

? Did the solution work? (Answers will vary.)

Students should be able to recognize that the addition of the plastic trees helped keep some of the sand from moving when they blew or squirted water on it.

explain

How Do Wind and Water Change Earth? Cloze and Read-Aloud

Connecting to the Common Core
Reading: Informational Text
CRAFT AND STRUCTURE: 2.4, 2.5

Using Features of Nonfiction

CCC: Stability and Change
Things may change slowly or rapidly.

Tell students that you are going to read a book that will help them learn more about how wind and water change Earth's surface. Share the cover of *How Do Wind and Water Change Earth?* and introduce the author. Then flip through the book to show the table of contents and some of the interior pages. *Ask*

? Is this book fiction or nonfiction? (nonfiction)

? How can you tell? (Answers may include it has a table of contents, photographs, bold-print words, and an index.)

Connecting to the Common Core
Language
VOCABULARY ACQUISITION AND USE: 2.6

Cloze

Pass out the Wind and Water Cloze student page. Student directions are as follows:

1. Cut out the cards at the bottom of the page.

2. Read the cloze, and fill in each blank with the card you think belongs there.

3. Listen carefully while your teacher reads the book *How Do Wind and Water Change Earth?*

CLOZE ACTIVITY

4. After reviewing the cloze as a class, move the cards if necessary. Then glue or tape them on the page.

5. On the back, draw an example of *erosion*.

After reading pages 4–19 of the book aloud, discuss the cloze and give students the opportunity to move the cards if necessary. Bring attention to the words *quickly* and *slowly* and how they are used in the cloze paragraph. Explain that some changes, like the ones caused by floodwaters (page 11), can be observed within hours. Other changes, like flowing water carving deep valleys (page 14), occur over a period of time much longer than one person could observe.

When students are satisfied with their choices, they can tape or glue the cards to the page.

> **CCC: Stability and Change**
> Things may change slowly or rapidly.

Next, have students draw an example of erosion on the back of their papers, and then have a few students share and discuss their drawings.

The completed cloze should read as follows:

Wind and Water

1. Wind, water, and ice can break large landforms into small pieces. This is a slow process called <u>weathering</u>. (page 4)

2. Air that moves is called <u>wind</u>. (page 4)

3. Moving material from one place to another is called <u>erosion</u>. (page 7)

4. Almost three-quarters of Earth is covered by <u>water</u>. (page 10)

5. <u>Floodwaters</u> can make big changes to Earth's surface quickly by moving rocks and carving out new channels. (page 11)

6. Rivers and streams can slowly carve out deep valleys with steep sides called <u>canyons</u>. (page 14)

7. When too much rain hits soil or sand, it can begin to slide away. This is called a <u>landslide</u>. (page 17)

8. Slow-moving rivers of ice are called <u>glaciers</u>. (page 18)

Erosion Problems

 *Questioning*

> Connecting to the Common Core
> **Reading: Informational Text**
> Key Ideas and Details: 2.1

Explain that erosion and weathering are happening to Earth's surface all the time. Sometimes these processes produce interesting and beautiful landforms, such as the Grand Canyon pictured on page 14. However, many times these processes are harmful to the land and people living on it. *Ask*

? What are some examples of harmful effects of weathering and erosion from the book? (floods, landslides)

? Have you ever seen any of the harmful effects of weathering and erosion in your neighborhood? (Students may have noticed flooded baseball fields, eroded streambanks, bare spots in their yards, etc.)

You may want to share some examples of erosion you have seen in your own neighborhood or around the school. Then show erosion time-lapse images from the internet (such as the ones at the following link) and have students discuss their observations and wonderings.

 www.usgs.gov/media/images/ coastal-erosion-san-francisco-3

Ask

? What could be done to repair this damage and prevent further erosion? (Answers will vary. Students will learn more about erosion control methods in the elaborate phase.)

 For more examples of erosion problems, project the following gallery: *https://lakeshoreguys.com/shoreline-erosion-photos*

elaborate

Erosion Solutions Journal

Explain that thankfully, there are many solutions available for erosion problems. Pass out the Erosion Solutions Journal student pages. It has space for drawing and writing about four different types of solutions for controlling erosion:

- Using **plants**
- Covering soil with **fabric**
- Installing **rock** or building retaining **walls**
- Constructing earthen or concrete **levees**

  (*Note:* These solutions are often used in combination with one another.)

For each page of the journal, read the solution together, then show a variety of examples using photos and videos. (Suggestions are in the chart that follows, but local examples would be ideal!)

> **SEP: Constructing Explanations and Designing Solutions**
> Compare multiple solutions to a problem.

LOCAL EROSION PROBLEM AND SOLUTION

Table 16.1 Erosion Solutions

Type	Examples	
Use **plants** to hold sand or soil in place	How Do Plants Prevent Erosion? (diagram) *https://socratic.org/questions/how-do-plants-prevent-erosion*	
	Willow Cuttings for Stream Erosion Control *https://bygl.osu.edu/sites/default/files/inline-images/Willow%20 Erosion%20Control%20-%20JB.jpg*	
	"How to Plant Dune Grass for Coastal Sustainability" (video) *www.youtube.com/watch?v=kDRuaF1H7XU*	
	"Wind Break" (video) *www.youtube.com/watch?v=95Slo2Fv3og*	
Cover soil with **fabric** to hold soil in place while plants grow through it	Jute Erosion Control Fabric *www.fisherbag.com/wp-content/uploads/2015/09/fisherbag-Jute-Erosion-Control.jpg*	
	Salmon River Bank Stabilization (erosion control fabric and plants) *www.intermountainaquatics.com/salmonriver*	
	The Kawainui Watershed Permanent BMP Project (plastic erosion control fabric over mulch and grass seeds) *www.stormwaterhawaii.com/portfolio/ kawainui-watershed-permanent-bmp-project*	
	Backyard Stream Repair (installation of erosion control matting) *www.youtube.com/watch?v=_qUWLMVBYY4*	

Continued

Table 16.1 Erosion Solutions (continued)

Type	Examples	
Install **rocks** or build retaining **walls** to hold soil in place	Riprap Shoreline Restoration (riprap rock over fabric) *https://lakeshoreguys.com/our-work*	
	Creek Bank Erosion Control (riprap rock over fabric) *https://reynoldscontractingva.com/creek-bank-erosion-control*	
	Rocks *https://tdhlandscaping.com/wp-content/uploads/2019/06/ Internal-page-Erosion-Control-Drainage.jpg*	
	Retaining Walls *https://bythewall.com/retaining-walls*	
Construct earthen or concrete **levees** on riverbanks to control flooding	"What Are Levees?" (video) *https://www.youtube.com/watch?v=X-pxokpBDvk*	
	Wikipedia Media File: Levees (click through gallery) *https://en.wikipedia.org/wiki/Levee#/media/File:Sacramento_ River_Levee.jpg*	
	A New Orleans Levee *https://image.cnbcfm.com/api/v1/ image/102945760-GettyImages-482149280. jpg?v=1529469328&w=630&h=354*	
	Earthen Levee on the Ohio River *https://kgs.uky.edu/kgsweb/download/misc/landuse/UNION/ unionissues_files/image016.jpg*	

As you show examples for each type of solution, discuss the following:

? How does the solution control erosion? (Answers will vary.)

? What do you think are some advantages, or positive things, about the solution? (Students may note that the solution seems safe for people, animals, and the environment; uses natural materials; seems inexpensive or easy to use; is nice to look at; and so on.)

? What do you think are some disadvantages, or negative things, about the solution? (Students may note that the solution could harm people, animals, or the environment; seems expensive or difficult to use; would take a long time to work; is not nice to look at; and so on.)

Next, have students draw a picture to represent an example of the solution and record their observations and wonderings in their journal.

Encourage students to look for erosion solutions in their own neighborhoods. Maybe they have seen people putting down fabric or noticed retaining walls. Perhaps they live near a levee or have heard of one nearby. They may even have erosion solutions, such as wind breaks, rock walls, and drainage ditches filled with gravel, around their own homes.

evaluate

Comparing Solutions

 *Writing*

Connecting to the Common Core
Writing
RESEARCH TO BUILD KNOWLEDGE: 2.8

After students have filled out the first four pages of their journal, read the following scenario from page 5 of the journal:

Mr. Weathers has a problem. There is a stream running through his yard. The stream is getting wider every year. What should he do?

 (If you would like to project an actual photo of this scenario, you can find it here: *https://content.ces.ncsu.edu/media/ images/Figure_2-highly_erosive.jpg*)

Ask

? Why is this a problem for Mr. Weathers? (He is losing his yard, and the water is getting closer to his house.)

> **SEP: Constructing Explanations and Designing Solutions**
> Compare multiple solutions to a problem.

Next, have students study the drawing, then answer questions 1–5:

1. How is this problem an example of erosion? (Students should be able to explain that soil is being carried away by the water in the stream.)

2. Think about the different erosion solutions in your journal. Which solution would be best for solving Mr. Weathers' erosion problem? (Answers will vary, but students should be able to name a reasonable solution from their Erosion Solutions Journal.)

3. Why did you choose that solution? (Answers will vary, but students should be able to describe an advantage of the solution or explain why it is a better choice than other solutions.)

4. What might be a disadvantage, or negative thing, about that solution? (Answers will vary, but students might cite the high cost or difficulty of installing the solution, risks to wildlife or the environment, how the solution looks, how long it would take to work, etc.)

5. Draw on the picture to show the solution being used.

A Local Erosion Problem

In order to give students an opportunity to apply what they have learned to a real-world local erosion issue, locate a place in your community that has an erosion problem. If you are unable to take the students to observe it firsthand, take photographs and/or video to share with your students in the classroom. You can use the questions from the Mr. Weathers scenario to guide the discussion. *Ask*

? Why is this a problem? (Answers will vary.)

? How is this problem an example of erosion? (Students should be able to explain how soil is being carried away by wind or water.)

? Think about the different erosion solutions in your journal. Which solution would be best for solving the erosion problem? (Answers will vary, but students should be able to name a reasonable solution from their Erosion Solutions Journal.)

A LOCAL EROSION PROBLEM

? Why did you choose that solution? (Answers will vary, but students should be able to describe an advantage of the solution or explain why it is a better choice than other solutions.)

? What might be a disadvantage, or negative thing, about that solution? (Answers will vary, but students might cite the high cost or difficulty of installing the solution, risks to wildlife or the environment, how the solution looks, how long it would take to work, etc.)

> **SEP: Constructing Explanations and Designing Solutions**
> Compare multiple solutions to a problem.

If the problem is on public property, you may want to have students write letters to the local soil and water conservation district describing the problem and their proposed solutions. Alternatively, invite someone from your soil and water conservation district to your classroom to evaluate their solutions.

STEM Everywhere

Give students the STEM Everywhere student page as a way to involve their families and extend their learning. They can do the activity with an adult helper and share their results with the class. If students do not have access to the internet at home,

Opportunities for Differentiated Instruction

This box lists questions and challenges related to the lesson that students may select to research, investigate, or innovate. Students may also use the questions as examples to help them generate their own questions. These questions can help you move your students from the teacher-directed investigation to engaging in the science and engineering practices in a more student-directed format.

Extra Support

For students who are struggling to meet the lesson objectives, provide a question and guide them in the process of collecting research or help them design procedures or solutions..

Extensions

For students with high interest or who have already met the lesson objectives, have them choose a question (or pose their own question), conduct their own research, and design their own procedures or solutions.

After selecting one of the questions in the box or formulating their own question, students can individually or collaboratively make predictions, design investigations or surveys to test their predictions, collect evidence, devise explanations, design solutions, or examine related resources. They can communicate their findings through a science notebook, at a poster session or gallery walk, or by producing a media project.

Research

Have students brainstorm researchable questions:

? What is topsoil and what is it made of?

? What was the Dust Bowl?

? What can farmers do to protect their topsoil from erosion?

Investigate

Have students brainstorm testable questions to be solved through science or math:

? What observations can you make of soil in your area?

? Can you change the course of a river using pebbles? Make a model.

? Does the slope of a hill affect the shape a river makes when running down it? Make two models using soil or sand and compare.

Innovate

Have students brainstorm problems to be solved through engineering:

? Can you build a model of a house located on a riverbank?

? Can you design and model a solution to protect the house you built from a flood?

? Can you design and model a solution to protect the house you built from a dust storm?

you may choose to have them complete this activity at school.

Websites

Websites are listed within lesson.

More Books to Read

Hyde, N. 2016. *Earthquakes, eruptions, and other events that change earth*. New York: Crabtree Publishing Company.
Summary: This book explains that although most of Earth's surface is changed slowly over hundreds or thousands of years, some changes happen quickly in a matter of minutes, hours, or days. These fast changes include earthquakes, landslides, volcanic eruptions, and tsunamis. Includes full-color photos, a glossary, an index, bold-print words, a hands-on activity, and diagrams showing the layers of Earth and how mountains are made.

Hyde, N. 2016. *Protecting Earth's surface*. New York: Crabtree Publishing Company.
Summary: This book reveals the ways Earth's surface is constantly being changed by wind, water, and human activity, and it describes how people can reduce the detrimental effects of these forces by planting trees and grass, installing plastic soil covers, and building levees. Includes full-color photos, a glossary, an index, bold-print words, and a hands-on activity.

Pattison, D. 2019. *Erosion: How Hugh Bennett saved America's soil and ended the Dust Bowl*. Little Rock, AR: Mims House.
Summary: Set in the 1930s during the Dust Bowl, this story of soil scientist Hugh Bennett describes how he used his vast knowledge of soil composition, erosion, and land management to convince politicians that the soil needed help. In the end, his hard work paid off and Congress passed a law establishing the Soil Conservation Service, the first government agency dedicated to protecting the land.

Storad, C. 2012. *Earth's changing surface*. Vero Beach, FL: Rourke Educational Media.
Summary: Simple, spare text and full-color photos describe both quick and slow changes to Earth's surface. Includes bold-print words, comprehension questions, a glossary, an index, and websites.

Name: _____

Wind and Water Cloze

1. Wind, water, and ice can break large landforms into small pieces. This is a slow

    process called _____.

2. Air that moves is called _____.

3. Moving material from one place to another is called _____.

4. Almost three-quarters of Earth is covered by _____.

5. _____ can make big changes to Earth's surface quickly by

    moving rocks and carving out new channels.

6. Rivers and streams can slowly carve out deep valleys with steep sides called

    _____.

7. When too much rain hits soil or sand, it can begin to slide away. This is called a

    _____.

8. Slowly moving rivers of ice are called _____.

landslide	floodwaters	erosion	glaciers
weathering	canyons	wind	water

National Science Teaching Association

Erosion Solutions Journal

What is erosion?

Wind and water can move Earth materials like sand or soil from one place to another. This is called erosion. Erosion can cause many problems. Let's explore some solutions!

Name: _____

Plants

Erosion Solution: Use plants to hold sand or soil in place.

What do you notice?	What do you wonder?

National Science Teaching Association

Fabric

Erosion Solution: Cover soil with fabric to hold it in place while plants grow through it.

What do you notice?	What do you wonder?

Rocks or Walls

Erosion Solution: Install rocks or build retaining walls to keep soil in place.

What do you notice?	What do you wonder?

National Science Teaching Association

Levees

Erosion Solution: Construct earthen or concrete levees on riverbanks to control flooding.

What do you notice?	What do you wonder?

Comparing Solutions

Mr. Weathers has a problem. There is a stream running through his yard. The stream is getting wider every year.

1. How is this problem an example of erosion? _____

_____

2. Think about the different erosion solutions in your journal. Which solution would be best for solving Mr. Weathers's erosion problem?

_____

3. Why did you choose that solution? _____

_____

4. What might be a disadvantage, or negative thing, about that solution?

_____

5. Draw on the picture above to show the solution being used.

National Science Teaching Association

Name: _____

STEM Everywhere

At school, we have been learning **how wind and water can change Earth's surface**. To find out more, ask your learner questions such as:

- What did you learn?
- What was your favorite part of the lesson?
- What are you still wondering?

At home, you can watch how a civil engineer studies the damaging effects of wind.

 www.pbslearningmedia.org/resource/b9199698-8a69-4468-b224-8bbcab0c7531/b9199698-8a69-4468-b224-8bbcab0c7531

Available in English and Spanish.

After watching the video, discuss the following questions:

1. How did the engineer model the effects of wind damage on a wall and a car door?

_____

_____

_____

2. What would be fun or interesting about this job?

_____

_____

_____